THE AMAZING SPIDER-MAN

THE BOOK OF EZEKIEL

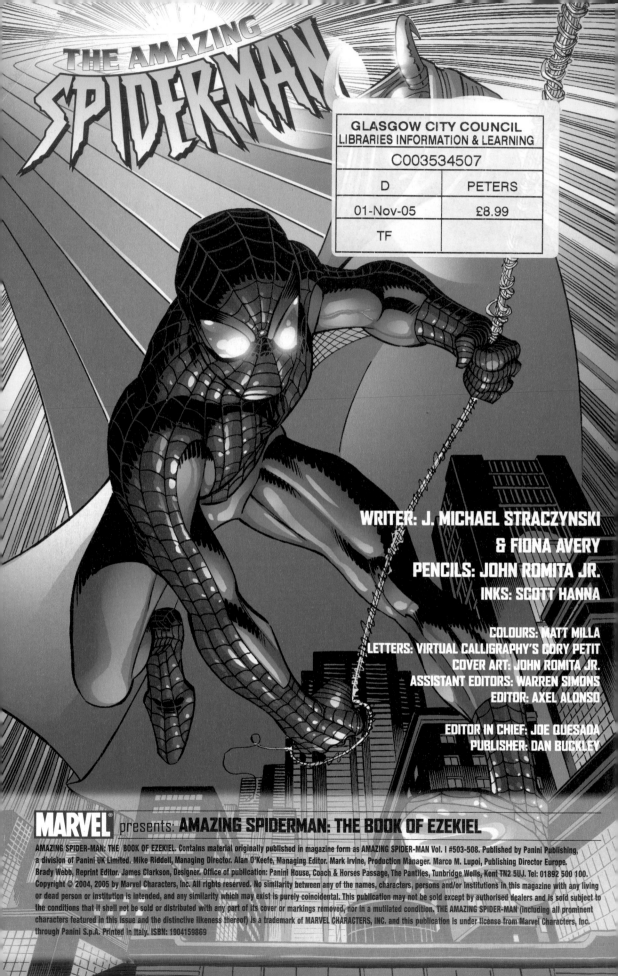

THE AMAZING SPIDER-MAN

WRITER: J. MICHAEL STRACZYNSKI

& FIONA AVERY

PENCILS: JOHN ROMITA JR.

INKS: SCOTT HANNA

COLOURS: MATT MILLA
LETTERS: VIRTUAL CALLIGRAPHY'S CORY PETIT
COVER ART: JOHN ROMITA JR.
ASSISTANT EDITORS: WARREN SIMONS
EDITOR: AXEL ALONSO

EDITOR IN CHIEF: JOE QUESADA
PUBLISHER: DAN BUCKLEY

MARVEL® presents: AMAZING SPIDERMAN: THE BOOK OF EZEKIEL

AMAZING SPIDER-MAN: THE BOOK OF EZEKIEL. Contains material originally published in magazine form as AMAZING SPIDER-MAN Vol. I #503-508. Published by Panini Publishing, a division of Panini UK Limited. Mike Riddell, Managing Director. Alan O'Keefe, Managing Editor. Mark Irvine, Production Manager. Marco M. Lupoi, Publishing Director Europe. Brady Webb, Reprint Editor. James Clarkson, Designer. Office of publication: Panini House, Coach & Horses Passage, The Pantiles, Tunbridge Wells, Kent TN2 5UJ. Tel: 01892 500 100.

I knew it was coming. I tried to pull away, but I was stuck.

BA-DOOM!

You shouldn't be here! Your presence is changing the dynamic of the spell. Get out! Get out while you still--

Stuck. Even as it moved toward me, away from them, on the day Times Square went mad.

Faster, searching, feeling, bending, yearning, faster... it fell upon me...

...bore down upon me with eyes of shadow and night, eyes I could not see, only feel.

But it could see me, could want me. But why?

AAAUUUGGH...
GNNNNNNN...!!

Why me?

Hunnzzhh....

I don't know how long I was unconscious, but I knew it wasn't safe.

I had to get home, away from the chaos and the danger, and a sense that something had changed.

That everything had changed.

"Heimdall, ever faithful, guards the Rainbow Bridge from anyone coming or going without the Allfather's permission. Even when he is being bored by conversation with that fool Volstagg, he misses nothing.

"And yet...many times have I fooled him using powers known only to a few in my family. For Odin was not alone in hanging upon the Yggdrasil Tree for fourteen days to learn runes. I too lost precious life blood to the study of dark arts.

"The runes never lie. They have an uncanny way of knowing just what disguise I need to delude my Asgardian brothers.

"But even so, this is a most interesting choice ..."

A Valkyrie, a Titan and Jesus walk into a bar...

Cool move. How'd you--

CHINK!

--whoa!

Well... nuts.

You know, normally this could crimp a guy's style. But not--

--your friendly, neighborhood Spider-Man.

Now, you want to tell me what the heck you think you're doing, lady? Is there a webbing shortage, or--

Hey! He's getting away.

He is not important.

The Spider-Man is here, I can feel him.

And I feel something more, the same presence I felt before. Is he the key to what I am seeking?

Hey, kid, you know you're talking to yourself, right? Gotta watch that or you'll end up like me, and--

Silence, mortal.

I wish to thank you.

Thank me? Can we back up a second? What part of thanking me is letting one of the bad guys get away? I don't even know you, so how can--

Not long ago, you released me from an ancient bondage that nearly destroyed me.

Look, lady, your lifestyle is none of my business, so--

There was a great battle between worlds. In that battle, you became my savior.

I really don't have time for this. I gotta try and pick up that guy's trail, get something to eat, and my favorite cartoon comes on in half an hour, so--

You fell through time, you and the other, Doctor Strange.

How could you--

Ah, now I have your attention. How could I know unless I was there, unless I had access to a greater wisdom than you seem willing to acknowledge. I felt you fall, and followed your trail of life from deep within my prison of darkness. You released me and I found new life here. I must show my gratitude for this.

No thanks are necessary, I'm just--

You do not understand. I must repay you. You cannot decline.

Look, lady, I'm not the one you want to thank, it's ...

Whoa, Peter, hold on, don't send the Doc any trouble he doesn't need. Let's find out what's going on first, then I'll run it past him.

On the other hand, I don't want to be rude, so...what kind of "thanks" are we talking about here?

I will give you the world. Such is my ability.

Ma'am, I don't *want* the world. I couldn't handle the world. I couldn't even manage Brooklyn.

Then again, who can?

Besides, I can't just go saying yes to strange women on the street-- not that you aren't quite interesting in a... translucent sort of way, but--

I will give you a night to decide...

"...Either accept my answer, or be destroyed by the power that I possess."

Boy, talk about people who won't take no for an answer. First Shathra, now this nutbar.

Maybe it's me. Maybe I attract these kinds of women. If I do, what does that say about me?

Maybe I can get the Doc to write a book. "Fifty Ways To Be Successful and Say No to Homicidal Interdimensional Cuties."

Tony Robbins, eat your heart out.

Yo, Doc, you there?

Holy--

FIRE! FIRE!

Someone call the police.

Is anyone in there? Are you hurt?

Perhaps if you will not stay at my behest, you may stay to prevent the death of someone else.

Oh my God...

Exactly.

NO!!

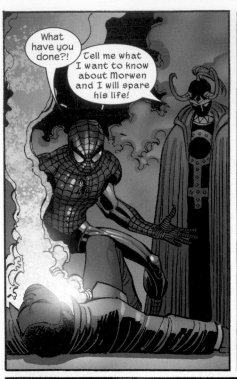

What have you done?! Tell me what I want to know about Morwen and I will spare his life!

Hold on! Hang on!

He only has a matter of minutes left to live. Tell me you will stay with me and I will save him.

You can't just--

Can and will. You may carry him to safety, but give me your word that you will stay by my side, or I will allow him to die.

I can't, I...all right. Fine. I give you my word, I'll come back!

Very well.

Runes of life and blood, touch this mortal...

...And restore his life in the name of the All Father and the Sacred Tree.

I almost expected him to weasel out of the deal somehow, but he did as promised. I got the guy as far away from the god as I thought I could.

Even thought about breaking my promise to Loki...but if he kept his side, how could I do less than him?

The only way to defeat Morwen is to drive her from the body she currently occupies. Unfortunately, the force of such a separation could drive the host body insane, or even kill the one that carries her.

That's not an option. Whoever she took over, she's innocent in all this. We can't let her be killed over this.

Death frightens you. Doesn't it?

No. Meaningless deaths offend me.

I see. Interesting.

Because you have kept your word, and because you are no real threat to me, I have a proposition for you.

In order: Yes, I did, yes I am, and I'm not interested.

Let me try this another way, I...apologize.

You? Apologize? You?

Look, I'm sorry, but if you've been possessed by the spirit of a Boy Scout, there's nothing I can do to help you.

Well, except teach you some camp songs--

I offer my help, since your friend Doctor Strange is unavailable.

What makes you think I will trust you at all?

You don't need to trust me. You can simply work alongside me if you choose not to work with me. But I ask that you do not interfere with me in facing Morwen.

Do we have a deal?

Yes. On the condition that no one else dies.

Good.

The mortals call this place The South Bronx.

I believe it may be sufficient to my needs.

BLATTA

BLATTA

BLATTA

Too many of them --augh!

BLAM!

It's no good--we gotta bail! They're gonna kill us all!

No, they will not kill you.

I will protect you. And give your weapons the power to overcome anyone in the world... tonight.

Our guns!

Wicked!

This is but a start, a warm-up, for I have far to go, and much to do, before the end.

Because all things must come to their respective ends.

Even the world itself.

"So this is, as you say, the finest your city has to offer?"

Hey, it's a hot dog. You know anything else that says New York more than a good dog with mustard, maybe a little chili?

I'm just not altogether sure you've given this a great deal of thought.

Could be. See, I've been thinking, and it's odd...lately I've been handling more than my share of magic cases.

I mean, usually it's some guy in a powered suit, or a piece of technology, or bio-engineering...magic, not so much. Until lately.

Some days I think I'm being set up for something.

I share the feeling.

--is there a chance that she could survive having Morwen yanked and still end up with all her neurons still pointed north?

Yes... yes, there is. I have...an idea.

I knew you would.

How about this?

If the Spider-Man doesn't want the power you're offering, I will happily take it and work with you. If it's all about gratitude, surely the assistance of a god is superior to that of a mere mortal.

This by you is an idea?

Being of assistance is not the reason I want this man. My role as sorceress is to serve the forces of chaos. Only through chaos does a race grow stronger.

The Spider-Man is a born agent of Chaos.

Yeah, I get that all the time.

Long have my masters watched him. There is much of the trickster in him, much of chaos...much of the spider.

But I'm the GOD of trickery, how much more chaotic can you get?

At what point, exactly, did this conversation turn into the supernatural version of American Idol?

Just asking.

Get clear!

Loki?!

I sometimes wonder...what ever happened to honorifics? Once upon a time, it used to be Sir Loki, Loki-your-honor, even Mr. Loki would suffice...

They went out the year Kennedy refused to wear a hat for the Presidential Inauguration.

What...?

Nevermind, long story. Just listen to me!

I have no wish to kill you, Spider-Man. But if you keep helping that godling, I will have no choice.

Let's try this another way... let me take her on directly and you just stand back.

She's far more powerful than you. You cannot win against her.

That's the thing. I don't need to.

I realized that Morwen didn't know Tess was your daughter until *after* she was inside her. That means she didn't choose Tess for her godlike abilities.

Go on. Tell me in this way...

Maybe it was something in Tess, something godly in her, that called out to Morwen!

You have to fight.

I'm afraid. I can't!

Come to me.

Come to me. Show her how wrong she is. Show her your strength, my daughter. That a father's angers can still be found in a daughter's eyes. That anger is something to be feared.

Father!

NO! I will not let you!

FATHER!

Come to me!

I have to kill you.

Is she going to live?

Yes. She is in a deep sleep of forgetfulness now.

So...where do you and I stand...now? I mean...

I owe you a favor, for saving her life. One day, should you choose, you may collect upon it.

Under the usual conditions, of course.

Cool.

...I think.

Doc Strange still wasn't in town, so I did a little investigating of my own at the public library.

There was nothing on microfiche or any literature on Morwen, First Sorcerer of Chaos.

I looked her up online too. All I got were X-rated sites. Thankfully the public library has a block on that stuff. Talk about embarrassing!

Shopping | Money | People & Chat

Search ▷ Morwen + Sorcerer of Chaos

Then I did some checking on Tess Black.

Doesn't seem like Loki' kid. For starters, she' respectable, even mac the paper a few times She's a stock trader an pretty well-off.

I put her home phone number into the new feature online and got a map of her address. I think the service is stupid--stalkers could have a field day--but it's handy for a guardian angel like myself.

Oh, and I made absolutely sure Aunt May's number stayed unlisted. Just 'cuz.

I stop by the house but...

It's for sale. I wonder if I have the right place.

Checking in?

PRESENTED BY
MASTRO
Realtors

Oh, it's you.

That's "Sir You the Mighty" to you. And when you address me, it's His Holiness and please and thank you.

Well, then, Your Royal Terror, would you please march right over to a comfortable chair and take the time to explain this "For Sale" sign on Tess' home. And please tell me how Tess is doing.

Tess has no memory of the conflict, which is the best thing for her.

Yeah. That's good.

She also has no idea she's the daughter of an Asgardian God.

But you're going to tell her, right?

I have no intention of jeopardizing my progeny with enemies or foolishness because they discover too much of their origins.

This is all of Tess' vital information, including where her new home is located.

Cool trick.

I want you to look after her, make certain she doesn't remember what happened with Morwen. You would do that for me, right?

So much for the favor of the gods.

Tess
Spring St.
12 555 6612

My request has displeased you?

Nah, it's just...I have my own reasons to look after Tess anyway. Morwen might be back to try and take over her body again.

That is my concern as well. And that's one thing we finally have in common.

Yeah. You weren't a big fan of street pizza or hot dogs.

If you need me, use the rune. That rune you have will summon me in an instant should Tess be in danger.

Right. Kinda like Loki Phone Home.

What?

Nothing...

But I kept the Rune. Then headed home after my patrol, thinking that it's kinda cool to have a god on your side, all things considered.

We apparently have the same glands, but to a much weaker extent. Although lately, that's been challenged. Which is the point I was just getting to...

Peter--

A human being can smell only a few molecules of musk, and even smell ants. Did you know that's where the word *pismire* originally came from?

Peter--

So that whole "vibes" thing may really *be* something. Even schizophrenics have this unfamiliar odor caused by a certain acid exuded in their sweat--

Peter.

I'm gonna be late. We need to say our good-byes here since they won't let you into the gate with me.

I was hoping I could just keep talking and if I kept on talking...I wouldn't have to *say* any good-byes.

That sounds kinda crazy.

Yeah well, the last time we said good-bye, you know, it kinda hurt. And I'm a little worried that *this* time, if we say it--

No, we'll say, "*See ya later,*" instead. And I expect a goodnight call promptly at midnight--every night-- don't forget.

Then we won't say good-bye.

We won't?

I won't forget. I'd have to be thrust into the fiery chasm of the abyss where there's bad cell phone service before I wouldn't call you for good night.

See ya later, then.

See ya, Tiger.

Two weeks earlier....

--and like I said, I need to get back to my career now. An offer has come in, a big offer. It's something I can't pass up.

I understand. So long as things are fine with us.

Everything is fine with us. I'm ready to go back to work knowing that you'll be here waiting for me when I get back.

Why am I so reasonable?

I wouldn't mind except sometimes I'm unreasonably reasonable.

So I decided to bury myself in the work, knowing that if I just sat around, I would miss MJ. I would worry. In other words, I'd be stupid.

But it's a happy-skippy night. Seems like everyone's behaving just when I need some rowdiness.

I wonder how MJ is doing.

BEVERLY HILLS, CALIFORNIA.

It's three hours earlier in L.A., but I bet she's feeling New York time nonetheless.

Baramont Pictures

This is the biggest break in her entire career. I feel weird not being there.

You look good as new. Now, smile for me.

Go knock 'em dead, girl. This is your big day.

Excuse--

Excuse me--watch out!

Sorry...

Can I *help* you?

I have a five o'clock with John Parson.

And *you* are...?

Mary Jane Watson-Parker. I'm here for the role.

Oh, uh...

if you'll just wait one moment...

I'll call him and let him...*know.*

Yes, MJ is here to see John, I...I know, but--

--well, then *you* do it. Fine, I'll come back there and see him myself.

One moment, please.

...Well she's here and she doesn't know about John being gone or that you already hired Pamela Cartman. What do you want me to do about it?

I don't care how you get rid of her. She was Parson's choice and it's not my fault he didn't follow up after he was fired. But we're not going with her so send her away.

But what do I tell--

Tell her I don't want some bimbo model with delusions of talent in this role! It's too important!

I'm sorry, can you--

Hello? MJ?

Twelve-twenty-five? No...

Twelve-forty! No...

Oh, I always forget I'm upside down...

Hey, what's doing?

You wanna get off the roof?

Only if you share a fry.

So, what's going on?

Oh, it's nothing. Nothing we need *you* for.

Looks like a stakeout to me.

And in lieu of your excellent observational skills you are going to blow it hanging around.

So what are you staking out?

Um...

Mmm foftrifm. mmm.

I can't hear you.

It's...

Someone is stealing bicycles. A female undercover just rode in a bike and hooked it up here.

And we're waiting for the culprit to nab it so we can arrest him.

That's--

Very--

Very thoughty of you.

Okay-okay! It's a nothing assignment. But we gotta do what we gotta do, right?

Right. Well, seeing as it's rather slow for me too, I'll help you guys out.

‡Heh-heh‡

‡sigh‡ Great.

I never believed it when they said people in L.A. can kill you with a smile on their face.

How could they have fired John Parson without telling me or my agent? I came all the way out here for nothing. No, I came here to be insulted. Am I really just a model who thinks she's an actress? Delusions of grandeur...?

What am I going to tell Peter? I can't... I just can't tell him. I'm so ashamed.

What am I *doing* here? Nothing.

Nothing yet.

Just a minute, guys, I have a call to make.

Spider-Man has a cell phone?

Who do you suppose he's callin'?

BRRRINGG
BRRRINGG
BRRRINGG
BRRRINGG

The guest you are trying to reach is not available now. Please leave a message after the beep...

BEEP

Hey, it's me, calling to see how you're doing. You there?

Oh, it's a hotel phone. Even if you were, you wouldn't be able to pick up.

Hmm. Okay I'll call back a little later. Worried about you though. You can call if you get in-- it's slow tonight.

K-CHKK

That kid's gotta be 12 at most. Way too late for him to be ou---

AUGH!

Spidey Sense--calling--collect--again! The pain the pain! But *why*? What's so bad about this situation?

Who's there?

I ain't afraid of no one.

You hear me?! No one!

Something...about that kid... it's splitting my head in two. I don't understand. Why is my Spider sense going off about him? He's only 12.

I'd better follow him, just to be sure.

FREEZE!

What--!

Now I see why my spidey sense went nuts on me.

And if I don't move fast, this could escalate--

--into something ugly.

Gotta warn the cops first.

STAY BACK!

They're adults, they have some sense at least...

And now to take care of the kid...

Without anyone getting hurt by the gun...

What the--

Fingers stuck!

--myself included!

Gotta be careful, knock him down without hurting him--

Oof!

It's okay...it'll be okay--

No! Don't move!

But he's armed!

I said *stay back!* I mean it, guys! Don't blow this one!

Nuts...if I don't let go, it could go off...

KEEP AWAY FROM ME!

No. I'll go after him. *Do not chase him.* You'll only make it worse.

I move fast.

He's on the run, darting in and out of back alleys and through fences. Anybody could come out of those back doors.

This just got a lot more serious.

He's veered again. Nuts...

Where'd he get off to?

He's my responsibility now. I can't lose him!

Oh. There he is.

Worst place he could be. Forward, he falls, backward, he'll shoot. If I try and web him, he could shoot or fall.

I'll have to do this the hard way.

Hey... how's it going?

What--

Stay back! Stay back, I mean it!

Just thought I'd come by, check out the view. Nice night, isn't it?

Perfect for hanging around, target practice... surrendering your gun....

"...And never, ever let them see that you doubt yourself."

What can I get for you?

Club soda.

Coming right up.

I didn't order this.

On the house. It's miso soup, guaranteed to cure anything.

Probably a good idea... I haven't eaten all day. Thanks.

No problem. And I promise I won't ask for your autograph.

Hey, about time. So tell me the good news.

Good news...?

About the *part*. They offered it to you, right?

I... Yes, but...the pay was bad and the part just...it wasn't right for me. So I turned it down.

Aww, that bites. But you're right to say no. Makes 'em want you all the more later.

Are you all right? You sound kinda quiet.

Oh, I'm just tired. It was a long day.

I understand. Get some sleep. You've got a long flight ahead of you.

I will. See you when I get in, tiger. Was your day okay?

Somewhere in Peru....

I knew you would come tonight. They wanted to protect me, but I said it would do no good. That you would come regardless.

Did you--

They'll live.

Good. Then there is still hope for you--

--Ezekiel.

For a little while, at least.

I'm burning up.

I know.

You have to help me.

Inca blood flows in my veins. The blood of kings. Of Pachacuti and Inca Roca. When all this was known as Tiwantinsuya, a place of secrets. A place of power.

I am a descendant of kings. I do not *have* to do anything.

I will help you because I *choose* to help you. For what you have done to help my people.

And in sadness for what will happen to you.

Don't write me off yet, Miguel.

Others have tried before, but I always survived. I will survive this.

Perhaps. But understand: I will help you this one time more, but then you cannot return. If you try, I will not be here, and the door will be closed to you. But--

I must do this, because if you return again, you will not be as you are now. And either you will die... or I will die.

This is the last.

I'm sorry.

Just...do it. The bleeding. Bleed it out of me, out of my system, enough to buy me the time I need.

And then?

And then... I'll do what I have to.

He'll help me. I've worked hard to make sure of it. He'll help.

You mean he will die, do you not?

Just do it, all right? Just... do it.

You cut the man...you bleed the spider. You cut the spider, you bleed the man.

But when the blood is gone, the man is gone--

--and only the spider remains.

RRRRRRRRRR!

HONK! HONK! HONK

Mauro's

That's one down, now to--

No!

PARK

EEEEEEE!

SHUTTUP! SHUTTUP!

Back off, freak!

I just want to--

I said back off!

I'm taking her and I'm walking outta here, you got that?! You try anything and she's dead!

HONK! HONK! HONK! HONK! HONK! HONK! HON

Sorry... 'scuse me...coming through...bad guys to catch...

Nice dress, lady.

You ever think about washing that car, pal? What do you think this is, Jersey?

'Scuse me! Coming through!

I can't let you do that.

You got no choice!

PARK

Please, I--

I said shut up!

Look, you want a hostage, fine, take me. I won't put up a fight, you can put the gun right up to my head, and--

What're you, kidding?

Everybody knows bullets don't do squat to you, man! You're...what the hell's that word...invul...

Invulnerable?

Yeah, that's it, invulnerable.

Where did you get *that* idea?

Back off, man--

Look, I'm *not* invulnerable. I want to know who's putting this out there because it really hurts my value as a hostage, and I can't afford that, not in this economy.

Just got to keep him talking until I'm a little closer...can't risk webbing the gun...if it goes off--

I'm not telling you again...back off or I kill her!

You think I'm kidding?

Huh? That it? *You think I'm freaking kidding?!*

CLICK!

Ungh!

BLAM!

FFFFFFF!

AAAAIIGH! What the--who the heck--

"Depends. Does ordering in from Domino's count as cooking?"

"Absolutely, P."

--and there were three very nice hats, and they were just similar enough that I couldn't choose between them.

Now, perhaps it's just me, but if I were running a hat company, I'd want to make my products different enough that you'd want to buy all of them, instead of making them so similar that you feel foolish buying this one *and* that one because *this* one has a red ribbon and *that* one has a blue ribbon.

Not that I own a lot of hats to begin with, and I wasn't looking to *buy* two hats in any event, but it's the principle, isn't it, Mary Jane?

And then these little people from Venus showed up and not only did they cut in line, they bought up all the pink hats when everyone *knows* it's not pink hat season on Venus. That's the rule: no white shoes on Earth after Labor Day, and no pink hats on Venus after July.

Isn't that right?

Uh, huh... I...

...wasn't... listening.

I'm sorry, May, it's--

I understand. You've clearly got a lot on your mind right now.

Is it anything you want to talk about?

When I went to L.A. for the movie, they... they didn't want me for the role. They said they didn't want some model with delusions of being an actress.

I told Peter I turned the job down, I just couldn't...I couldn't, that's all.

But I've been wondering... are they right?

Actors are paid to walk and talk and be dramatic. Models are paid to sit still, shut up, and be distant. We're talking here about two different skill sets. Maybe I don't have it. Maybe I should just be what I am, do what I've done.

Yes. Please.

Would you like my opinion?

The film roles you've done so far...in one you were the beautiful girlfriend who was in jeopardy, in another you were the beautiful girl who tempts people to their death...in another you were the beautiful woman who inspires the hero...

It seems to me they hire you because they need someone beautiful to fill a niche in the plot, not because they want someone who can act.

You haven't played a character, MJ, you've only played things that move the story ahead.

I know. Which makes me think maybe I'm expecting too much... maybe I'm shooting too high. Is that possible?

Yes, Mary Jane, it is.

But it's also just as possible that you haven't shot high *enough*.

I left that newspaper behind on purpose, incidentally.

That sound like a natural ability to you? Or something closer to prescience? Precognition? Remote viewing?

Or are you saying you really do have eight tiny spider-eyes in the back of your head, beneath the hair where nobody can see them?

Don't even think about it, MJ.

Just checking. How many fingers am I holding up?

You do know you have to sleep with me, right?

Three.

Slappy says hello.

...redrum, redrum....

I...think I'll clear my place while you two work this out.

I can seeeeeeeee you...

Keep this up and you only *think* you'll be sleeping with me tonight, pal.

You know, MJ, Jeff Goldblum only picked up the genetic traits of a *fly* in that movie and it was really scary...

...can you imagine how much scarier it would've been if he'd been in that teleporter with a *spider*?

I am *so* going to hurt you, Peter.

"Thank you for the lovely dinner."

My pleasure. Nothing but the best take-out for a friend of Peter's.

Speaking of which...want to take a walk, P?

Sure thing.

Be back in a few, MJ.

One thing, Mary Jane... whatever Peter may think, I do know a few things about destiny. And about power.

We have as much power as we choose to have. And I have the power to see things...things that happen.

I see you on the stage. I see you before an audience. And I see your every doubt removed forever.

I'm never wrong, you know.

What was that about?

Were you ever a Boy Scout, Peter?

Yeah, but what does that--

"Just doing my good deed for the day."

What you have to understand is that power has three components.

Those that want it.

Those that give it.

And the final component, those who control it. The gatekeepers.

The spider is your totem. Real totemic power comes through supernatural channels. But the way you got your power circumvented that. Which wasn't so bad, as long as the gatekeepers didn't notice.

But now that I've been noticed--

The bill is coming due.

I told you that you were going to go through several trials in terms of supernatural forces arrayed against you. I told you that the worst of them, Shathra, was not the last.

And that there was one more coming. The most dangerous of all.

And I'm guessing you didn't come all this way to tell me he's been held up in traffic.

I'm afraid so, P. He's coming. The Gatekeeper is coming. Maybe even tonight.

Gotcha!

Heh...*that'll* teach you ta mess around with Lightnin' Jack, fastest spider-smasher in this part of--

--hunh?

WHAM!
WHAM!
WHAM!
WHAM!

Holy...

LEMMEOUTTAHERE!

"I know you've had a long night, Peter, so maybe the best thing is to just sleep in tomorrow."

I have to get up early, but I'll try not to wake you.

Why? What's up?

I...have an audition.

"An audition? Here in town? That's great, I didn't know they were shooting anything--"

"They're not."

It's... don't laugh, Peter--

I won't, I promise.

It's an audition for a play. It's just a little thing, Off-Broadway, over on West 7th, but it's a serious play, and I think it might be good for me, and--

"Peter, I said don't laugh--"

"I'm not laughing, MJ. I'm smiling."

I think it's a great idea. And long overdue. Let 'em see what you can do for real, as an actress, not just someone people drool over in magazine layouts.

Which, of course, includes me.

You're not just saying that? You mean it?

I've never meant anything more in my entire life.

"I think it'd be a great thing for you to--" "MJ?"

MJ? What...what's wrong?

I don't know, I...

There's something inside me. Something *inside* me...

Peter... help me! Help me!

"Oh my God..."

MJ? MJ!!!

...the pretender... beware the pretender... a price must be paid...

RRRRRRRRRIIIIIII

MJ!

-IIIINNNNGGGG

8:30

Yeah, I'm awake who--

Ezekiel? What--

Where the hell are you?

8:31

Turn on the TV.

Which channel?

I think this'll be on pretty much *all* of them, P.

Holy...

--the most astonishing sight I've ever witnessed.

CLICK!

Of course Spider-Man is responsible for this!

But Mr. Jameson, we know the Bugle has an anti-Spider-Man agenda--

Look, lady--

--if there were ten million ants crawling up West 7th, you can bet your diploma I'd be trying to get my hands on Ant-Man for a confirm-or-deny...

West 7th...?

That's where MJ was heading for her audition!

"So what brings you this far off Broadway, Mary Jane...?"

Well, I--

I mean, a *model* of your *stature*, all the magazine covers, the glamor, isn't this just a bit...déclassé? A bit off the beaten track?

I saw the audition notice. I read the script. It's a great script. I think I could do a good job with it.

My assistant explained that there are no lingerie scenes anywhere in this play, right?

Yes. Twice.

All right, fine then, let's get this over with.

Yes, make it a latte, three sugars, lots of chocolate and cinnamon, and be sure to get one of those mug snugglers, otherwise it burns my hands.

Go on, Mary Jane, go on, we're all watching.

And I said to her, I said, Ruth-Anne, that man is never going to marry you. He talks good, but he's like one of those billowy clouds you see out on the ocean, big and full of wind but they disappear as soon as things get hot.

What you want is a man of character. A man who will stand by you when other men would run. A man who--

Thank you, Mary Jane, I think that will be--

But there's another two paragraphs. I was barely getting started--

Yes, well, my mother had a car that started about the same way on cold mornings...all that awful noise, and--

...oh my Goddddd...

Unghhh!

Is everyone all right? Is anyone hurt? Is--

Oh...

Coming through!

Wait... I don't... holy...

Hold that thought--

Hey good-looking. So, what do you think of my family?

Yeah, we get that a lot.

Yick-yick-yick-yick-yick!

I think everybody got out okay, but I can go back and check. Who was that?

A director. He was mean to me.

Look, a puppy in trouble.

Go get him!

You sure you'll be okay from here?

I'm fine...they'd have to get a taxi to get here before I'm long gone.

So what're you going to--

I'm going to find out what's at the center of this by...

Well, going to the center of it.

You sure that's a good idea?

Mmmnnnnnope. But I have to start somewhere.

Catch you later, MJ.

Good luck. When this is over, you can find me in the shower. For the next four days.

Copy that.

Have to find the epicenter of all this, because that's where--

P...over here.

Ezekiel?

I wanted you to see this yourself. I told you something like this would happen. The Gatekeeper is down there somewhere, and he's not going to rest until he finds you. The only way to stop this is to get out of town...come with me--

I can't.

You can't help them by staying. You'll only make it worse--

Yeah?

EEEEEEEE!

Tell *her* that.

Hellllllp! Somebody, help meeee!

Pleeeeeeasse!

Don't move--

I'll have you out of here in a second.

Thank you, I--

Not a problem.

Boy, if I were one of you guys, I'd be real embarrassed to be stuck in a human-web. Now get gone before I tell your wives, and you know what'll happen then.

She'll bite your head off.

Uh-oh.

Did you just say uh-oh?

Uh-huh.

Nuts.

You know what? You don't look so tough to me. Just one more big strong guy.

Made out of spiders.

Well, okay, two points for originality.

Let me guess...you're the Gatekeeper, right? Well, if you're looking for the keymaster, he's in another movie.

Ghostbusters.

C'mon, everybody in New York's seen it, it's mandatory or they take away your driver's license.

Now comes the *real* test.

MJ was right...yick... now, I--

Whoa... okay, back off...I said back--

But...I don't understand...if all this is...if this is true...why are you...I thought--

It was necessary, that you might see the truth. See the pretender.

See... with the eyes of a spider.

"What you are doing is dangerous. I ask you again to reconsider."

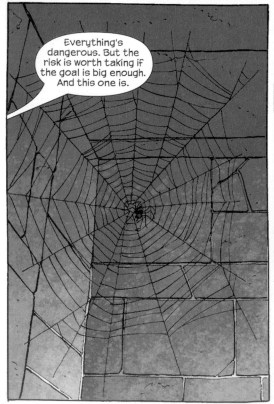

Everything's dangerous. But the risk is worth taking if the goal is big enough. And this one is.

If you take from the spider that which is not yours to take, one day a price will be asked in return.

To this generation, there is one chosen. You are not that one.

But I can *make* myself that one.

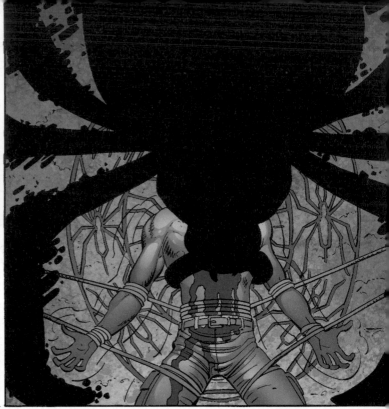

"When that time comes, Ezekiel, your only hope is to divert the powers you have bargained with, to bring them to attack the chosen, and in so doing eliminate your competition.

"Or, failing that, to convince him to fight them on your behalf...and bring him here, to the beginning, to this place...that his blood may take the place of your own when the madness, and the death, follows..."

Unhhh... unhhhhhHHHHHHH--

--HUUCCCHHH!

Lungs working again... I can breathe...some kind of drug...induced hallucinations....

But if any of that was true...

That's why Ezekiel wanted me to come with him to South America...maybe it's why each of the supernatural forces I've fought came the same time he showed up...he was trying to get me to fight them on his behalf...

When they were never really after me in the first place. They were after him. If that's true, then as long as I don't go to South America, I should be--

Hello, P.

How did I-- Yes--

Ezekiel.

Came to me...came to me in New York, tried to talk me into coming to South America...said the supernatural menaces that had been coming after me were coming again, hard--

--but he was lying. They weren't coming after me. They were coming after him. He used--

--used me.

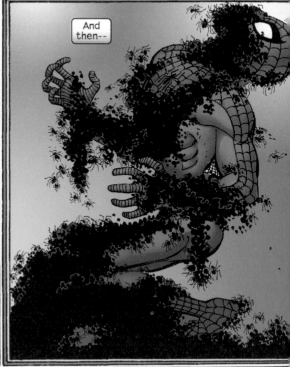

And then--

--then darkness, and the voice--

--the voice, old, so old--

--so cold--

--the hunter--

Blood is the milk of the world.

--the truth--

--your only hope, Ezekiel, is to divert the powers you have bargained with, to bring them to attack the chosen, and in so doing eliminate your competition. Or, failing that, to convince him to fight them on your behalf--

And the trap.

"--and bring him here, to the beginning, to this place...that his blood may take the place of your own when the madness, and the death, follows."

And then... here.

It's my life or yours. And I intend to live. But for what's coming, and how you'll go, I am sorry, P. Honest and true.

Tired or not, confused or not, I should have run the second I opened my eyes--

--stupid--

Ezek- Ezekiel? I don't want to fight you, I--

I don't either, P.

Don't fight it, P...you'll only hurt yourself. It's a neural toxin, designed to slow your reflexes to a crawl...you can't fight it.

Can't breathe-- burning up--

I lose the mask... doesn't matter... not here....

Just come with me...I don't want this to hurt more than necessary.

I don't want to die... not here, not now....

...not like this. In the dark. In the dirt.

Not like this. Not like this.

...not like this...

My blood for yours.

Your life for mine. My life for yours.

Now they will come-- the powers will come-- for my blood, my life, and they will find you.

And they will take you. And be satisfied.

And I will be free.

Goodbye.

Ezekiel, wait... Ezekiel--

EZEKIEL!

Nothing... I've never done anything...I had the power, but I never...

What was it for? What was any of it for? What--

AAAAGGGH!

...Peter...?

My God, what have I done...?

He's dead.

Yes.

Many times when he came to this place, he spoke of being a hero someday. But that day was always the next day, never this day.

He wanted the power to change the world. But he never used it because he was too busy...and because he did not understand.

Didn't understand what?

That he had that power long before he ever came here.

We think we cannot change things. We are wrong. We do not lack for power, or influence, or money.

All we ever miss...is the moment of decision. At the end, he had his moment.

At the end... what else is there?

We must get you to a doctor. I--

There was nothing I could do. He beat me.

Do you truly believe that?

Yes.

Then you are a fool.

Well. There you are.

Wait a minute...I mean, we barely... shouldn't we at least say something?

A man's life is his statement.

He needs nothing more from us.

Okay, great, maybe he doesn't, but I do.

I still don't know the truth. I mean, all this...the spider the way I saw it in there, the spider the way I...the way it happened to me--

What's the truth? The magic, or the science?

Tomorrow the sun will come up.

You can tell me all the reasons of science that it *does* come up, the orbital mechanics, all the laws of thermodynamics.

And I can say that it *will* come up because it is *meant* to come up.

I see no contradiction.

Do you?